When Love Takes Over

A Celebration of SGL Couples of Color

DARIAN AARON

iUniverse, Inc.
Bloomington

When Love Takes Over
A Celebration of SGL Couples of Color

iUniverse books may be ordered through booksellers or by contacting:

iUniverse
1663 Liberty Drive
Bloomington, IN 47403
www.iuniverse.com
1-800-Authors (1-800-288-4677)

ISBN: 978-1-4620-1393-7 (sc)
ISBN: 978-1-4620-1394-4 (e)

Printed in the United States of America

iUniverse rev. date: 5/20/2011

This book is dedicated to every lesbian, gay, bisexual, and transgender person who has ever been made to feel less than or out of arm's reach of the love of another or themselves.

"God is love...and love is for everyone."
-Archbishop Carl Bean

Acknowledgements

My baby has been born! It has been a long journey to get this book from inside my head to the page and finally in your hands and I have so many people to thank.

First and foremost I'd like to thank God for giving me a sense of purpose and direction. It has been very few moments in my life when I didn't know exactly what I was being called to do, and in those moments of uncertainty, he provided clarity.

To my parents, Drewey and Shirley Aaron, thank you for always supporting and encouraging me even when I made choices that you didn't necessarily agree with. I will forever be indebted to you for giving me life and unconditional love that overflows like a fountain.

To my sister, Delisha Finch and the world's greatest brother-in law Samuel Finch, thank you for loving and embracing all of who I am and giving our family the most precious gift ever in my nephew DeMaree and the newest addition to our family arriving in the fall.

To my best friends who have stood by me through all of the ups and downs, Bennie Taylor, Travis Davis, Albert Lee, and Alicia Christian. Thank you for always understanding and supporting me even when I was clearly losing my mind. You've loved me through all of my stuff and I'm eternally grateful.

To my new best friend and the love of my life, Joseph Gates. Thank you for showing up and allowing me to experience the kind of love that I'd only written about before you. I probably would have tucked this project away for a long time and surrendered to "I can't and never will" if it hadn't been for you.

To my amazing editor Asim, thank you for not turning out to be the ruthless editor I'd imagined you'd be, who would return my manuscript with never ending corrections in red ink. You handled my book as if it were your own and reassured me that my work was special and deserved a place in the universe.

There have been so many people who have influenced my career as a writer and activist. I would be remiss, not to mention a few people whose work and friendship lit the fire for what has now become my life's work.

Keith Boykin, my life changed the moment I picked up One More River To Cross in my local Books-A-Million Bookstore in Montgomery, Alabama. Your words spoke to me and for the first time I knew I wasn't alone and my life was not a mistake. Thank you for always being a positive example for me and countless others who dared to follow in your footsteps.

The late E. Lynn Harris, gone but certainly not forgotten. If someone had told me that I would have the privilege of personally getting to know one of the most prolific writers of our time, whose books I used to sneak and read as a closeted and scared young boy living in the Bible belt I would have said, "get outta here!" Your words of encouragement continue to propel me forward even in death.

Terry Angel Mason, I'm convinced that God knows exactly who to place in your life. Thanks for planting the seed for this book. We both knew that this book needed to be written and each time I doubted my ability to bring this project into fruition (which happened frequently) you were there to get me back on track as only you can.

To all of the bloggers, activists, authors, journalists, filmmakers, and radio hosts whose tireless efforts to bring attention to the stories important to the black LGBT community and who have supported Living Out Loud with Darian and now this book…thank you!

Rod McCullom, James Earl Hardy, Maurice Jamal, Patrik-Ian Polk, Pam Spaulding, Terrance Dean, Clay Cane, DJ Baker, Adrian Daniel, Drama

Dupree, Lonnell Williams, Andre Allen, Tron Majette, Ryan Lee, Ramone Johnson, J. Brotherlove, Rashid Darden, Adolph St. Arromand, Dwight Powell, Bernard Tarver, Derrick McMahon, Lee Hayes, Quincy LeNear, Deondray Gossett, Angela Bronner, Michelle Garcia, B. Scott, Michael Brewer, Craig Washington, Darlene Hudson, Brian Slade, Yolo Akili, and Anare' Holmes.

And last but not least, I'd like to thank every couple included in this book that were unafraid to love despite a cruel world that constantly reinforces the idea that it's wrong and impossible for two black men to love each other for a lifetime. You inspire me and I have no doubt your stories will inspire countless others.

Always live out loud!

Praise for When Love Takes Over: A Celebration of SGL Couples Of Color

What is so powerful about black love is its strength, beauty, and power. Darian has done a superb job in showcasing this with his amazing images of black gay love in this fantastic and prolific book, When Love Takes Over. What a wonderful tribute in celebrating 'us' and showing 'us' what it looks like, and how it can be done!

– Terrance Dean, best-selling author Hiding In Hip Hop; Straight From Your Gay Best Friend; Reclaim Your Power; and Visible Lives

"Pioneering in nature, bold in its intent while refreshing to the senses, When Love Takes Over is not just a celebration of male couples-of-color but it is a vivid, candid and an insightful journey into the intricacies of romance, love and commitment as expressed through the lives of eighteen couples.

Further, this book provides hope, guidance and a new way forward for generations to come on how to navigate meaningful, romantic relationships between and among men. Finally, for every male couple-of-color represented in this book there are literally tens of thousands in communities large and small not mentioned but who indeed exist and who share the same fabric of love. We must recognize them and embrace them as part of our families and our lives.

---Herndon Davis, Media Host/Analyst and Author

"Gay relationships are many things and they come in many forms. They are in constant motion, constantly evolving, but there is nothing more beautiful than two souls uniting. Love is boundless and we are all worthy of it. What a marvelous celebration of the beauty of our relationships!

- Lee Hayes, MPA
Author of the novels Passion Marks, A Deeper Blue & The Messiah

When Love Takes Over: A Celebration of SGL Couples of Color achieves an awareness of pure love that binds us as Black Gay Men and propels us to persevere and endure the superlative homophobia present in our society. These compilations articulated in this single piece of genre augment the hope and manifest the certainty that God's love is available to all. These men show through their ordinary life and work that love can be enjoyed by all. Indeed "Blest be the tie that binds."

-Rev. Tommie L. Watkins, Jr.
Author, Living Out Loud

"*When Love Takes Over: A Celebration of SGL Couples of Color* is a first of its kind, celebrating an overlooked group in the LGBT community. However, its focus of love transcends race and sexuality, people from all backgrounds can appreciate the book's sincerity and storytelling."

-Clay Cane
Journalist, BET

Foreword

Terry Angel Mason, Author of Love Won't Let Me Be Silent

One of my favorite quotations hails from the French philosopher, Voltaire, who uttered the famous words "There is nothing more powerful than an idea whose time has come!" And this book is another fascinating example of an idea whose time has definitely come!"

Darian Aaron has beautifully captured and chronicled the passion, the joy, and the magic of true love that has been experienced by 18 same-sex couples. The result of Darian's endeavors is a compelling masterpiece that romantically inspires and emotionally engages the reader. Darian pulls back the curtain of time and takes us into the hearts and minds of the 18 couples, as they share with us, their journey to romantic fulfillment from beginning to end. Moreover, this literary chronicle of true love vindicates and validates the desires of same-sex couples in wanting to fully participate in the American Dream which promises all citizens "life, liberty, and the pursuit of happiness" e.g., THE RIGHT TO MARRY THE LOVE OF THEIR LIVES!

Darian Aaron wisely documents the love stories of these 18 couples with a journalistic elegance and simple sophistication that allows the warmth and unique magic of each couple's story to unfold and engage the reader without being overshadowed by the author's ego. This literary ability sets Darian worlds apart from most contemporary writers and gives us, the reader, a timeless literary treasure that showcases the positive examples of same sex love. It is my fervent hope and impassioned prayer that this book will inspire and motivate other couples to aspire to and emulate the couples represented in this book who boldly and bravely declared their love to each other and to the world, refusing to surrender to societal and familial pressures, vowing to remain true to each other because LOVE TOOK OVER!

Introduction

"It's impossible for two black gay men to sustain a long-term relationship." If I had a dollar for every time I've heard someone utter this statement I'd be a wealthy man. This persistent notion that the potential to experience true love between two black gay men would be more like a scene ripped from the pages of an E. Lynn novel disturbed me. Having spoken to other black gay men, many had unfortunately accepted this destructive narrative as their fate. They were single, lonely, broken-hearted, or were connecting strictly on a physical level with potential partners while completely dismissing the possibility of having their heart's desire fulfilled.

I knew I had to do something! I had to be a part of changing the story that someone had manufactured and sold to us that the American dream, as seen through black gay eyes, was distorted, dysfunctional, down low, downtrodden and hopeless. One phone call to my good friend, mentor, and constant supporter Terry Angel Mason would ignite the spark for an ongoing series profiling black gay couples in committed relationships on my blog; Living Out Loud with Darian (www.loldarian.com), which resulted ultimately in the book you are reading now.

"You have a platform and the ability to change the way the world views us and the way we view ourselves," said Terry during our phone conversation.

"So many of us don't believe that we can have meaningful relationships because we don't see healthy examples of couples that are in love and are making it work," he added.

This was my call to action. Author and Pulitzer Prize winner Toni Morrison once said, "If there is a book that you want to read and it hasn't been written yet, then you must write it." It was growing increasingly unacceptable for me to continue complaining about the lack of positive examples of black gay men, in both the mainstream and gay press, when I possessed the wherewithal to make a difference.

When Love Takes Over: A Celebration of SGL Couples of Color is not a novel. I may eventually get around to writing one in the future, but this book is an extension of the passion I have for real stories involving real people. It is my dream that this coffee table book will find its way into the homes of millions of black same-gender loving people, where it will be placed proudly next to Ebony and Jet magazines to be seen by every single relative and visitor that you welcome into your home. But most of all, I hope this collection of black gay love stories inspires you in your own life, as it defies every myth and stereotype about who we are and what we've been told that we cannot achieve as black same-gender loving men if we allow love to take over.

Darian Aaron

Table of Contents

Part One

That's The Way Love Goes

Damien Ramsey & Seanmichael Rodgers

"Of course it was Damien's idea to get married, but it was me that took him to Tiffany. He picked a ring, and I got on one knee and asked him to marry me."
–Seanmichael

Location: Brooklyn, New York

Together four years. Married March 21, 2010 in New York City.

It was a simple, yet flirtatious message sent by Seanmichael 35, to Damien 30, on the social-networking site Myspace that started it all. An unconventional storybook romance never before recorded, much less appreciated by the masses, yet existing in bold colors and breathtaking illustrations.

"We dated for about two months, before we mutually decided to say that this was something that we both were willing to make work," says Damien.

The spark between them was undeniable, they knew it and soon everyone from family and friends to total strangers would know it too.

In between date nights; a weekly Tuesday night event according to Seanmichael "Where we shut down all business and focus on our love for one another." It was apparent that the love they'd hoped for had arrived and so did the journey towards learning and loving one another despite their differences.

"It takes two strong men to look at each other in the face of difficult times to say we are worth it and how do we make this work. Our backgrounds are so different and dialogue alone has been a major challenge, we received marriage counseling and that gave us the ability to redirect negative energy and learn to communicate our needs to each other".

And it was two strong men who vowed publicly on March 21, 2010 to love, honor, and protect one another before a standing room only audience on Manhattan's lower west side.

"I vow to emphatically love and radically love and comically love you. I vow to ambitiously discover your immaculate design and understand the passions of your heart and mind. I vow to care and protect you with all that is in me so you can have everything and anything you'll ever want or need. I vow to humbly and graciously hold your hand so wherever we are together we'll stand."

Shelton Stroman & Christopher Innis

"We tell people the same thing we tell our son and even he understands the basic premise. Children need a loving family and the world is made up of different types of families. We believe strongly that the success of raising a child has nothing to do with the parent's sexual orientation but more so based on instilling good values in the child."

Location: Snellville, Georgia

Together ten years

The definition of family is greatly expanding and Christopher Innis 36, and Shelton Stroman 38, along with their five year old son Jonathan is just one of many same-gender loving couples of color who have extended their love to include children.

The love and stability provided by Jonathan's two dads in a state that doesn't fully recognize or support gay and lesbian families is without a doubt cultivated from the love Christopher and Shelton shared with each other in the years prior to Jonathan's arrival. Thankfully, the wisdom of a friend would set the inevitable romance in motion.

"We met after a mutual friend thought we'd be a perfect match," says Christopher. "We spoke on the phone twice and immediately hit it off, so we arranged a date."

"We became good friends before we became lovers," says Shelton. "I admired that Christopher wasn't just interested in sex alone and was willing to take it slowly with the relationship. I think we were both cautious since we'd both had unpleasant experiences in previous relationships, yet caution didn't stop us from moving in together three months and a few dates later."

"I guess you could say the relationship moved pretty rapidly once it became clear that we had similar aspirations", says Chris. "Shelton was also very supportive in my coming out phase which only strengthened our bond. He was always more confident in his sexuality and came out to his family while in college and with his encouragement I found the strength to come out to my traditional Caribbean family. It was a process but when the storm cleared both our families embraced us with open arms and were thrilled to have a new addition to the family when Jonathan was born."

"We actually tried for one year to adopt kids through the foster care system in Georgia but faced numerous rejections from social workers because we're a same-sex couple," says Shelton. "We finally decided to go the private adoption route and within one week of an employing an adoption agency we were matched with a birth mother and were off to witness the birth of our son in a Louisiana delivery room."

"Having a child has changed our lives", says Chris. "We believe strongly that the success of raising a child has nothing to do with sexual orientation of the parents but whether or not they're capable of instilling good values in the child."

"Gay and lesbian people have families and their families should have legal protection. Banning same sex marriage is a form of gay bashing and it would do nothing at all to protect traditional marriage." –Coretta Scott King

Tony Harper & James Abernathy

"See, we've accomplished something that a lot of straight and gay couples haven't: we live together, work together, drive to work together, eat lunch together, travel together, shop together and have partied together for the last ten years and we're still together." –Tony

Location: Chicago, Illinois

Together ten years

If you believe in soul mates or the idea that there's someone special out in the world for everyone to love and to experience the one euphoric high that we're all chasing in some form or another, the one emotion that is as necessary to human beings as the air we breathe; then when you find that love and it's seamless you nurture and protect it. This love feels easy and absolute, simply put: destiny.

This is a chapter in the life story Tony Harper 45, and James Abernathy 30, are writing for themselves.

"We met while crossing paths at a casino where Tony was working at the time over ten years ago," says James. "I think we both knew almost immediately there was something that just felt right between us but we didn't know what it was."

"I had no idea when we met that I was looking at the man that I'd still be in love with ten years later and perhaps that's why we proceeded with caution in the beginning," says Tony. "Although it wasn't long before James packed his bags and moved in."

"I saw something different in James than in previous men I'd dated and I believe my parents saw it too and quickly welcomed him into the family."

"Some of my relatives initially had reservations about Tony and some still do but I love him and that's all that matters," says James. " I believe that God has brought us together."

"That's why we are committed to focusing on the positive and allow very little room for negativity to enter into our relationship", says Tony.

"Tomorrow is not promised so we never go to bed angry at each other. Our belief is if you want something bad enough it can be achieved together without any complications. We have ten years together and counting as proof."

Kurtis Sampson & Derrick Vaughan

"Kurtis and I both have strong individual relationships with God and because of that we have a solid foundation to stand on. The greatest contribution that religion has played in our relationship is the fact that we both believe that God made us for each other." -Derrick

Location: Atlanta, Georgia

Together three years; married on June 15, 2009 in Boston, Massachusetts

If the Internet is the new virtual coffee house replacing old fashioned meet and greets, then Derrick Vaughn 32, got a Grande' Latte' when he met Kurtis Sampson, 42, online over three years ago.

"We conversed for almost three months just online, checking on each other and seeing about each other's days," says Derrick.

"At the point when we finally exchanged numbers, our conversations were so smooth because we had gained such a connection with one another." What the pair didn't expect was to find a love that would transform their lives and ultimately destroy even the faintest doubt that a loving and committed relationship between two Black gay men wasn't attainable.

"We are one in the same," says Kurtis. " Our motto is "YDIFM" which stands for "You Do It For Me." "We are so equally yoked that it surprises us sometimes."

What has been joined by God let no man put asunder.

And after a surprise proposal from Kurtis complete with an emerald and diamond ring taken from his pinky finger and an enthusiastic yes from Derrick- within months the couple were bound for Boston, Massachusetts as two individuals who had previously led separate lives but would return home as one both spiritually and legally.

"The wedding was so intimate and real," says Derrick. "It's something that I will never forget."

"I'm not pulling any punches anymore. I'm black, gay, and I love the Lord and you can't take that away from me! You don't have to associate with me, but you can't take my God or my rights away because you don't agree with me."-Billy Porter

Daryl Edwards & Rodney Williams

"We just get along. We're perfect for each other. We never go to bed mad at each other…because whatever happens today, something worse can happen tomorrow. If it's not life threatening, we just move on."-Daryl

Location: Aurora, Colorado

Together nineteen years

If you were to look up the word longevity in the dictionary and discover Daryl Edwards and Rodney Williams' names being used in a sentence, it might come as a surprise but it wouldn't be entirely inappropriate.

Together for nineteen years, this Colorado couple defies the persistent myth…at least in some circles…that male same-gender relationships and specifically black male same- gender relationships are short-lived. This loving couple and their accompanying story of how love manifested itself in their lives, is what those opposed to same-sex unions would have you to believe is destroying the "sanctity of marriage." Daryl and Rodney have been together longer than most heterosexual marriages last and they are without a doubt made for each other. Daryl obviously knew it nineteen years ago when he took drastic measures to grab Rodney's attention.

"I'd seen him riding around at City Park in Denver and I tried unsuccessfully to get his attention," says Daryl. "So when I saw him at Cheesman Park later that day, I remembered his car and the hat he had on and I stood in the street in front of his car and told him he was either going to stop or run me over. He stopped and we started talking and that was nineteen years ago."

"We dated for about three months before we both decided that we wanted to enter into a serious relationship and we moved in together shortly thereafter," says Rodney. "We just threw caution to the wind and jumped right in."

"I came to Denver with a purpose," says Daryl. I wanted to find a job, a lover, and buy a house. I accomplished all that."

"Rodney and I will be together for twenty years soon and we both want to get married, although gay marriage is illegal in Colorado we are registered as domestic partners," says Daryl.

"We proposed to each other over eight years ago so marriage has been on our minds for a while, but it looks like domestic partnership is the closest we're going to get in Colorado for the time being," says Rodney. "Although we're not opposed to traveling to a state to wed where our relationship is fully recognized."

With nineteen years of love and commitment between the two one of the biggest lessons learned was the act of selflessness according to Daryl.

"My happiness is not as important to me as his happiness. I'm going to be happy but I'm going to do what I can to make sure he's happy. There's so selfishness in our relationship."

Deondray Gossett & Quincy LeNear

"Love is not the basis of a relationship. I can love him to death but if I don't respect his feelings or I am unable to set aside my own selfishness then the relationship is doomed. People put so much on love. I am certain that many men love their mates and continue to hurt them because they lack the other important ingredients."-Quincy

Location: Los Angeles, California

Together thirteen years. Domestic partnership May, 2010

Hollywood power couple Quincy LeNear and Deondray Gossett are well known for capturing the diversity of the black gay experience on screen through their award winning series The DL Chronicles, but their off screen narrative as partners in life and work is just as compelling. Together in love for over thirteen years it's almost hard to believe that one half of this inseparable duo never imagined the person he would commit his life to would be another man.

"My long term vision was that of a wife and children, says Quincy. "I had very heterosexist ambitions due to being socialized to deny my same-sex desires. I never thought it was possible then to be in love with a man. My perspective was changed and I had to reconstruct what my heart felt against what the outside world told me to feel or not feel."

On the set of an independent film that provided the opportunity for the two to connect, Quincy would gain an opportunity to ignore society's expectations for his life and follow his heart down a path that led directly to Deondray.

"I was still in a long distance relationship at the time with someone else who only wanted to be gay during his once a month visit, behind closed doors in my bedroom," says Deondray. " Quincy was supposed to be a one-night type of deal. But somehow I knew, even before we did the deed, that this was someone who had crept into my consciousness. He made me feel new, needed, and we were always laughing."

It wouldn't be long, six months to be exact, before circumstances would bring the pair together under one roof to begin writing the first chapter of a love story that has lasted well over a decade. And like every story that has had highs and lows, Quincy and Deondray are no exception, actually they are better because of the challenges.

"When there's an issue, we get it out in the open and deal with it," says Deondray. "It may sometimes involve cursing and screaming, but we're really always just saying, "Stay with me, damn it!'

Quincy and I will come right out and ask the question to each other, "Do you still want to be here?" And sometimes in the heat of passion we've yelled, "No!" As soon as the word flies from our lips, we are running to go catch it and swallow it back up. So far we've never meant it."

"After thirteen years I still wait by the door for him to come home when he's gone," says Deondray. "I still smile when I see him in the morning. He's my partner and best friend. I am totally content with just me and him and no one else around."

But after thirteen years together with no legal recognition of their relationship and the highly publicized setback of Proposition 8, the voter approved gay marriage ban in California, Quincy and Deondray were not content on celebrating another anniversary based on the day they met, they wanted and needed more. And while California's domestic partnership registry afforded the couple some of the rights and privileges of marriage it wasn't the same but would have to do in the interim.

"It was great, but it was quick and no more eventful than mailing off my taxes," says Deondray on the registry process. It was at that moment that I felt robbed. No raising of the right hand or anything. I had to do more swearing in for my passport. Suddenly my political opposition to Proposition 8 had become a personal one. I felt unequal and less- than under the law. This will have to change."

"It is not enough to tell us that one was a brilliant poet, scientist, educator or rebel. Whom did he love? It makes a difference. I can't become a whole man simply on what is fed to me: watered down versions of black life in America. I need the ass-splitting truth to be told, so I will have something pure to emulate, a reason to remain loyal." –Essex Hemphill

Part Two

The Body That Loves You

27

Jon & Mike-Mack Garrett

"When I met Jon he was so quiet, and by his mannerisms I assumed he was the type of gay man that was hyper-masculine and would think I was too effeminate for him. But after our first date I knew he was the one for me." – Mike

Location: Bowie, Maryland

Together two years. Married May 7, 2010 in Washington D.C.

If Jon Mack-Garrett 29, had any inkling that he would meet his soul mate and future husband Mike Mack- Garrett 33, at a bowling event that he'd been invited to several times over and declined to attend he may have laced up his shoes a bit sooner.

"I was ready for a relationship, but I had given up on it ever happening," says Jon. With the arrival of Mike any relationship uncertainty that existed prior to their first hellos would soon subside.

"I knew that Jon was going to be in my life for the long haul, but I was unsure if he felt the same way", says Mike. "So I just took it day by day and after two months we moved in together. I know some people thought we moved too fast, but in my heart I just knew that he was the one for me," he adds.

Mike's early intuition about the future of their relationship may have been a few steps ahead of Jon's, but Jon wasn't far behind and luckily for the future spouses neither was the support of their families.

"My family embraced Mike as their son-in-law, as soon as they met him," says Jon. "They have only met one other person I was in a relationship with. So for me to bring Mike home to meet them they knew this relationship was serious."

The seriousness of their relationship became crystal clear during a casual November stroll near the Jefferson Memorial in D.C., as Jon got down on one knee and proposed to Mike at the site of their very first date.

May 7, 2010 Jon & Mike publicly declared their love and commitment to one another in a legally recognized marriage ceremony in the presence of family and friends at City Hall in Washington, DC.

"As a gay man you just never think that you'd meet someone that you're so compatible with on so many different levels. I want you to know it's my mission in life to make you happy…to make us happy," vowed Mike.

"I vow to be there for you in your laughter and in your tears and in your sickness and in your health. I vow to protect you and never leave your side. I vow to keep good memories alive and let the bad ones die. I vow not to let the sun go down on our anger and to treat every morning as a new day to love you."

Jason Strong & Anthony Henderson

"We were pretty serious immediately. The only time that we have not physically been in each other's presence is when either one of us are away on business." My best friend said to me, "I give you six months and you guys will be living together." Well, it was six months and one day before we moved in."-Jason

Location: Los Angeles, California

Together five years

The traditional black church has always played an important role in the spiritual lives of the African-American community, but for many black same gender loving people it has been both a place of refuge and condemnation where negative messages regarding homosexuality and same-sex unions are as commonplace as Easter Sunday celebrations and mass choirs. So it's almost ironic that Jason Strong 35, and Anthony Henderson 33, first caught each other's attention during Sunday morning service, an hour where singles ministries are promoted and coupling up is encouraged if you're heterosexual.

"I was ushering and the pastor's wife invited Anthony," says Jason. "I remember staring at him the whole service to the point that I know he must have felt uncomfortable because I felt uncomfortable for paying more attention to him than to the message; however I swore I would get him."

"Jason walked past me about one hundred times to the point where I couldn't concentrate on the service," says Anthony. "I didn't think to much about it at the time until he walked up to my car two weeks later after we agreed to meet after our paths crossed for a second time on a phone chat line."

"When he pulled up to the front of my house and I saw him in the car I almost passed out! Shortly after he left we spoke that night on the phone until three or four in the morning," says Jason. "That's when I knew this was it."

What's Jason and Anthony's secret to a long lasting fulfilling relationship? Communication.

"No matter how mad we get, we both sleep in the same bed," says Jason. "As long as both parties are under the same roof things can be worked out. We're a couple that has been joined together and through faith believe we're meant to be together. Divorce is not an option for us."

"You have to go the way your blood beats. If you don't live the life you have, you won't live some other life, you wont live any life at all."- James Baldwin

Eric J. Parker & DJ Baker

"He was subtle and cool with his game and made me feel as if I was the only person in the room. I've never felt so vulnerable with someone I'd just met. DJ has a very loving way of engaging you in his conversations, especially when he's on his crazy rants."-Eric

Location: New York, New York

Together three years

The New York City socialite meets the gay activist radio shock jock. On the surface it may appear as if this recipe is merely an experiment on the validity of opposites attract, instead of the required ingredients for happily ever after, but what you sense when you're in the presence of DJ Baker 38, and Eric J. Parker 25, is an authentic love that reaches beyond labels, age differences, and societal expectations. A love that reverberates from private stolen moments shared just between the two to the eyes and ears of countless same-gender loving individuals whose capacity to remain hopeful that love will find them sometimes grows bleak. DJ and Eric remind us it's possible although even they may have been uncertain in the beginning.

"Eric's age was a problem for me in the beginning," says DJ. "But he was very mature and had such an intense passion for achieving his goals I couldn't help but be drawn to him."

"We met on the set of Vantage Point, a talk show DJ co-hosted," says Eric.

"He was so sexy and I walked up to him after the show and began talking to him," says DJ.

"We talked for hours on the phone that night and we connected instantly," says Eric. "Not in my wildest dreams did I think that phone conversation was going to lead to a long-term relationship. I just thought I'd give this guy a chance and see where it went. That was one of the smartest decisions I've ever made."

"We dated for two weeks and allowed ourselves to proceed with caution the first week," says DJ. "But by the second week we jumped right in once we realized how strong our feelings were for each other and made it official."

"Although I was very cautious considering the circumstances, I had to learn to let go and let love take over," says Eric. Needless to say, most of the obstacles we've faced have been imposed on us from family or outsiders. Honest communication is so important to our relationship and it's what continues to keep us together."

"Communication and great sex! And of course our date nights," says DJ. "Love is a risk that is not guaranteed, but a risk Eric and I have both been willing to take."

"Everyday we fall in love with each other all over again and trust that we're both committed to this journey."

Nathan Mitchell & Dwayne Jenkins

"We allow each other space to breathe and just as easily enjoy the time we spend together everyday. We laugh at one another on a daily basis, and try our best to check in, ask questions and listen. We respect one another and our investment in this journey we share." –Dwayne

Location: Nashville, Tennessee

Together fourteen years

When Dwayne Jenkins 45, and Nathan Mitchell 46, met in the spring of 1996 at a Nashville CARES volunteer meeting it was supposed to be all business. They were focused on creating a safe and affirming group for same gender loving black men in their area and weren't the least bit interested in finding "the one", nor did it ever occur to either of them that the one could only be a few feet away.

"Each of us was just getting out of four year relationships, and the thought of immediately jumping into another one was the last thing on my mind," says Dwayne.

It was literally a dare that set the wheels of this inevitable romance in motion, a romance that was clearly obvious to the men witnessing the connection developing between Dwayne and Nathan but somehow escaped the two people involved.

"One night after a meeting, we all got together at someone's apartment and ended up playing truth or dare. It was my turn and the "truth" question I accepted was; "Is there anyone in the group whom you are attracted to?" When I answered no, Nathan somewhat loudly stated to the person next to him, "Damn! He didn't even give any of us a chance!" I tried to back track, but someone shouted, "Oh don't try and change your answer now!" Later as we walked and talked ahead of the others to our cars, we were told everyone could tell it was a done deal."

"Honestly, after I asked Nathan out on our first "official date" to the 99 cents Movie Theater, I suspected we were right for each other. If a man doesn't mind you taking him to a cheap movie, and sharing the snacks you snuck into the movies, drinks and all, he's a keeper!"

"Within the first few months, we both decided to wear rings," says Nathan.

Like many states in America Dwayne and Nathan aren't afforded the right to marry in Tennessee despite their level of commitment.

"If we were able to get all of the same financial benefits that heterosexual couples have I would consider getting married," says Dwayne. "As it stands now, we've had three styles of commitment rings, a mortgage, and various other legal documents within our fourteen year relationship so it's safe to say that we feel more than legal."

"Each of us respects one another and our investment in this journey that we share. Beyond it all, we are best friends who truly cares for the well being of the other. Regardless of what the future holds, our friendship is the most important ingredient that keeps us together."

"Who has decided that my loving someone, who is a reflection of myself is a revolutionary act? What evidence do they have to prove it is, and if it's a revolutionary act, what is a black SGL man to do if he can't love another black man, and by extension love himself?" – James Earl Hardy

Derek Griffin & Phillip Lewis

"In black society as a whole we spend so much time looking at the expiration date on everything. I feel if you're always looking for something to expire and you never enjoy the contents or true shelf life of something, it does just that...expire. We as black men expect the end but never put forth an effort to prevent the end, but it's possible-look at us." -Derek

Location: Atlanta, Georgia

Together fourteen years

Love can find you in the strangest places and usually when you least expect it, but being open to the possibility of giving and receiving true love when it presents itself in a convent can be the key that opens the door to an amazing journey with your soul mate. Yes, I said a convent, as this was the case with Phillip Lewis 38, and Derek Griffin 34. But it's not the kind of convent you may be thinking...one filled with devout Catholic leaders in stiff habits, yet I'm sure the pulsating rhythm and energy experienced by Phillip and Derek over fourteen years ago inside Chicago's Convent nightclub was comparable to a religious experience. "He was the most adorable thing I'd ever seen," says Phillip. "He had on this fisherman's hat that looked like Paddington Bear and I told him he was attractive and I was going to make him my lover."

"I could feel him watching me," says Derek. "It just so happened that we had mutual friends that introduced us and the rest is history."

Little did the pair know at the time that their first test in what would become a life long commitment would come in the distance that separated them with Derek residing in Chicago and Phillip in Gary, Indiana.

"We dated for about six months and commuted to see each other and the more we talked and hung out the shorter the distance became," says Derek.

"On a whim we decided to pack up and leave our established lives as individuals and move to Kingsland, Georgia to start a life together. I swear that was the best decision we ever made," says Phillip.

"We were young when we started dating, but decided early in our relationship that breaking up was not an option," says Phillip. "It was a committed relationship in terms of us committing to argue until any problem we had was resolved. Go to sleep mad if needed, sleep in separate rooms if needed, but to always remain friends and stay together."

"When people hear how long we've been together they're always so shocked," says Derek. "I don't understand why since we've worked and continue to work at staying together."

"We recognize how fortunate and blessed we are and thank God for it every day," says Phillip. "I'm blessed to share a fire for God with Derek and believe our life together is a testament of our faith and relationship with him."

"I have come to believe over and over again that what is most important to me must be spoken, made verbal and shared, even at the risk of having it bruised or misunderstood."- Audre Lorde

Ricky & Cas

"The passage of Proposition 8 in California was disturbing. But to be perfectly honest, I know it is just a pebble thrown against the tidal wave of justice that cannot be stopped. Many people are afraid of change and they cling to religion and outdated morality out of fear of the unknown. Fortunately, there is a new generation rising that will not be consumed by fear and change will come... so we do our part by living as open and authentically as we can everyday."- Cas

Location: Los Angeles, California

Together seven years

It has been said that the idea of the traditional nuclear family consisting only of a mother and a father is a complete farce that has been sold and passed down throughout generations. One need only peer into the homes of African-Americans to witness children being raised by single parents, grandparents, aunts, uncles, and yes, even same-sex couples to know that this is true. Yet the notion persists that same gender loving couples in committed relationships that provide love and stability for children are somehow a threat to opposite sex couples and are doing a disservice to their children.

Well, Cas 52, and Ricky 34, along with four-year old daughter Jamaya refuses to be bothered by the naysayer. And despite the inequality of U.S. Immigration laws (Ricky is a Jamaican citizen) and living on opposite ends of the country in the beginning of their relationship-this would only prove to be temporary roadblocks for a couple who isn't afraid to fight for the happiness they so richly deserve and have found in each other.

"We first met at a bar on Christopher Street in the West Village in 2000," says Ricky. "We talked for hours non-stop and he was nice enough to walk me to the train station where we exchanged numbers and said goodnight. I smiled all the way back to Brooklyn. I knew there was something special about him. I wanted more but he lived in Los Angeles and I lived in New York."

"Ricky kept our friendship alive by calling every month or so when I returned home to Los Angeles after my business trip to New York," says Cas. "I had no idea he was interested in me and I was concerned that perhaps he was too young for me. Three years went by before Ricky made it to Los Angeles and his scheduled one-week visit turned into three weeks. A few months later he moved to Los Angeles to be with me."

"I guess you could say we didn't really date," jokes Ricky.

"I have kissed a few toads along the way, but I've found my prince, and he happens to be a man of Jamaican descent. Our relationship defies the myth one day at a time that two gay men of color can't have a successful union," says Cas.

"We work hard not to take each other for granted and to keep the lines of communication open," he adds.

"Immigration issues are a big obstacle but we try not to shout at each other when we have conflict, we sit down and talk about it," says Ricky.

"My sister and I were both born in the United States of America, both raised in the same house, by the same parents, and yet we don't have equal rights," retorts Cas. "My sister met a man from Jamaica, married him, and he was able to acquire citizenship and they were free to live as a family. Yet, I am not allowed to marry the man I love and offer him citizenship, therefore, my sister and I are not equal under the law. Those that try to differentiate between who deserves equality and who does not should be ashamed of themselves."

"We were very upset about them taking away our right to marry in this state [California]. But until marriage equality is granted on the federal level it really won't do us any good."

The thousands of rights and benefits granted to heterosexual couples that offer support to the family structure and are often taken for granted are legally denied to Cas and Ricky, and their daughter Jamaya. In a country that boasts the importance of family this is an injustice that must end.

"Our daughter is happy, healthy, beautiful, smart and creative due to her innate spirit and the support of two fathers who love her unconditionally."
"This is our reality."

"Sexual disposition parallels race. I was born black and had no choice. I couldn't and wouldn't change it if I could. Like race, our sexuality isn't a preference. It is immutable, unchangeable and the constitution protects us against prejudices based on immutable differences."-Julian Bond

Part Three

Love Will Never Do (Without You)

Michael & Jamil Smith-Cole

"Within the first year I asked him one day, if he'd ever thought about marrying a man and he said, "Yeah, I'm going to have me a wedding." And I said, "Okay." Afterwards we just let it die down, until one day I was driving and "You Complete Me" by Keyshia Cole came on the radio and that song moved me and I said, "Let's have a wedding. "And he said, "Okay." -Michael

Location: Atlanta, Georgia

Together three years. Married September 13, 2009 in Minneapolis, MN

If the black gay community has ever come close to having a married celebrity couple then Jamil and Michael Smith-Cole are it. The pair received national attention and became instant fodder for countless blogs when wedding photographs lifted from their Facebook profile went viral making them the unsolicited faces of black gay marriage.

But behind the unwarranted controversy and lavish wedding ceremony was a love affair that began two years prior.

"We saw each other from a distance in Piedmont Park during Atlanta Black Gay Pride. "I was in awe of him and I guess he was too," says Michael. "Apparently, we'd met at Detroit's Gay Pride earlier that year." "I saw him walking towards me and I remembered him from Detroit," says Jamil. "We were staying at the same hotel and we ended up talking the entire night."

"When I met Jamil I was 47 years old, so realistically speaking I didn't think it would be something long term," says Michael. "But I knew after our first night together wherever the relationship was going to take me I was willing to go. If it was just that night, a week, or a month or the rest of my life I was gearing up for it."

If you'd asked Michael prior to meeting Jamil if any same-sex relationship he'd had in the past or would have in the future would have the potential to lead him down the aisle his answer would have been a resounding no, but Jamil would become the person who changed that.

"I was heavy into church and they were constantly beating the idea into my head that homosexuality was a sin," says Michael. "But when I met Jamil he helped me come to grips with my sexuality and my spirituality-so marriage then became an option for me."

That option led to the ceremony that many have called "The Wedding of the Century," but it was the impact of Michael and Jamil's courage to share their love with the world that lives on even after that memorable day.

"Quite a few gay kids have come up to us with tears in their eyes and told us that we were living out their dreams. We hope that by them seeing us that they'll know commitment and marriage is attainable for them too. Many young black gay men have told us that they were going to begin to live their lives differently because they want we have."

Christopher & Dammeon Hicks-Marshall

"You can actually say that we sort of fell in love over the phone first, which prompted a great deal of anxiety, so we met the very next day, made love for three hours, fell further in love and immediately shut down our online accounts."
–Christopher

Location: Atlanta, Georgia

Together six years

One of the mistakes I believe same-gender loving couples make is to pattern their relationships after the heterosexual model that in many cases have proven to be unsuccessful even for opposite sex couples given the high divorce rate in America. Seeing this as a potential pitfall, Christopher Hicks-Marshall 40, and Dammeon Hicks-Marshall 36, are creating their own rules and have done so even from the beginning of their six-year relationship.

"I've often heard brothas say "If you find him on the internet that's exactly where you're going to lose him". Funny. I've never heard anyone say "If you find him in a coffee shop that's exactly where you're going to lose him." But what's great about Christopher and Dammeon is that they continue to defy the idea that their Adam 4 Adam romance would only be physical and never blossom into the mature and nurturing love they experience today.

"We didn't date. We exchanged a couple of e-mails and then we talked on the phone for about six hours," says Christopher.

"The next day we both left work early and decided to meet in person. There was this undeniable chemistry between us that led to hours of lovemaking," says Dammeon.

"It truly was love at first sight. It's an amazing feeling to meet someone who desires to have a healthy long-term relationship and also shares identical values."

"We don't feel like our honeymoon phase has ended despite being committed to each other for six years and facing the usual challenges that occur in relationships," says Christopher.

"There's a healthy and unhealthy way of resolving conflict and most of the time we choose to communicate with an open heart and listen without interrupting in an effort to come to some sort of compromise or resolution, even when we don't completely agree with one another."

"We can be defensive and argumentative too," adds Dammeon. But we always come right back around to communicating in a healthy way because we love each other and we are one."

"Despite marriage bans for same-sex couples in Georgia we both believe in the institution and champion for it to be legalized. The legal merging of our last names represents our oneness and a public statement of the lifetime commitment we've made to each other."

"I speak to remind you and myself that I can hold my lover's hand in Anacostia or Harlem or South Central or Oakland and I am not always found in Dupont Circle or Christopher Street or Santa Monica Boulevard or The Castro."-Keith Boykin

Rico Newson & Antonio Jones

"I believe one of the biggest obstacles in maintaining a healthy relationship is learning to love yourself and being comfortable with who you are. A lot of people (both gay and straight) are seeking validation from their partners but the love and validation has to begin within."-Rico

Location: Atlanta, Georgia

Together two years

In a city like Atlanta that is populated with over five million people and boasts one of the largest African-American black LGBT populations in the country, it's not unusual to hear tales of woe from single black gay men when it comes to finding a suitable partner.

The cycle of dating and investing time in a potential beau only to be left frustrated and with a broken heart can leave one jaded and completely closed off to the possibility of experiencing true love.

"I'm not doing relationships anymore!" How many times have you heard a friend or maybe yourself utter this statement? Well this is exactly what Rico Newson 41, said before Antonio Jones 28, came into his life and changed

"I'm not doing relationships anymore" to "I'm only doing a relationship with him."

"I had gotten completely comfortable and happy being single and then I met Antonio at a club," says Rico. "He was so aggressive that it actually worked at commanding my attention," he teases.

"I knew the first night we met at the club that Rico was the one for me," says Antonio. "We dated for a few weeks and I knew this was going to be serious. We spent just about every day together."

"Everyday together after the first night we met," Rico interjects. "He wouldn't come and see me the first night, he's been a respectable gentleman from the very beginning."

The simplicity of their relationship and their newfound happiness together may have come as a surprise to those around them but the timing couldn't have been better for Rico who had given up on ever finding his king.

"My friends were happy for me but a bit thrown as well because I'd given up," says Rico. When I met Antonio's family they immediately embraced me and welcomed me into the fold.

"I truly see Rico as my king and his happiness is just as important to me as my own, with that as our priority we make an effort to enjoy each other everyday so our relationship continues to thrive," says Antonio.

"It's been two years and we're looking forward to many more years together. We still date and as a couple enjoy experiencing all the new and exciting things life has to offer. Our relationship can go as far as we allow it."

Mikael & Davon Phillip-Chisolm

"One of the reasons we are happy can be contributed to being honest about everything and learning to let go of the little meaningless things. Another aspect of us being happy comes from the understanding that we both led separate lives before becoming one and still continue to have normal, healthy, social relationships with our friends and family"-Mikael

Location: New York, New York

Together four years. Married October 10, 2010

When it comes to matters of the heart it seems there's no shortage of "sayings" or colloquialisms disguised as pearls of wisdom to help someone get on with, get through, or get over love. "If it's meant to be it will be," "The moment you stop looking for love is the moment love will find you." If the love was truly real, it'll come back to you"…I'm sure you would agree that we could all line our pockets with cash a million times over, if we had a dollar every time these phrases were uttered."

But what would you do if the love you thought was within arms reach disappeared only to return years later? Would the circumstances surrounding cupid's trickery cause bitterness or would you open yourself up to receiving the blessing you narrowly missed the first time around?

Mikael Phillip-Chisolm 22, and Davon Phillip-Chisolm 28,was given the chance to answer that question after their paths crossed online in 2006 and after hitting it off Davon abruptly disappeared.

"I was fresh out of a five-year relationship and I was not ready to commit myself to another one, so I stopped speaking to Mikael," says Davon. "I didn't want Mikael to think he was a rebound guy and I didn't want to hurt him."

"As fate would have it about a year later, when I was doing my taxes I ran into Davon," says Mikael. "I was reluctant at first but we ended up going on a date. I let go of my anger and gave it a shot. It wasn't long after the banana pancakes that I had for dinner, along with the romantic backdrop of the snow falling, was when I began to remember why I liked Davon. I had a feeling after our first date that he was/is the one."

"We became inseparable," says Davon. "We would call and text each other all the time and by the fourth month Mikael moved in with me. Those close to us scrutinized us for moving so quickly, but we knew it was right and once our families saw how serious we were, they gave us their blessing, and four years later we're still together."

"Now we have our share of obstacles like any other couple, communication being the biggest, but we've learned that truly listening to each other helps us resolve this issue."

"I try to shift the focus and ask myself if I'd rather be right or happy? Happy always wins."

"We definitely have a habit of speaking our minds in our relationship and when we are in the wrong we acknowledge, apologize, and move on from the subject and it works wonders," says Mikael.

"I prayed and asked God to guide me to love and I found it in Mikael," says Davon. "I truly believe he brought us together. This is one of the reasons why being married is so important to us because it legally binds our love and commitment and will provide the necessary protections for our children when we have them."

"A boy, Logan, and a girl, Madison Li, we've already named them and adoption plans are underway," says Mikael.

"It's been four years and we're still attracted to each other mentally, physically, and emotionally. I can honestly say our love gets better everyday."

"I wish we would have had same-sex marriage thirty years ago to be perfectly honest. I think there would be thousands, perhaps tens of thousands of gay men who would be married and alive today if this society would have afforded them the same equality and the same normalcy and the same dignity as is afforded opposite sex couples." -David Catania

Michael Slaughter & EJ Flavors

"When we were younger there were many examples of committed relationships and surrogate family structures. It was a way of surviving in what was a much more hostile environment for black gay men."-Michael

Location: Atlanta, Georgia

Together twelve years

The idea that love happens when one least expects or isn't actively searching for it may sound a bit cliché', but it happens to be the truth for Michael Slaughter and EJ Flavors both 43, when vacation plans filled with sightseeing in New York City were altered as the two men set their sights on each other. That was twelve years ago.

"I wasn't even looking for a relationship," says Michael. "I was visiting from Oakland and EJ was visiting from Atlanta. We talked the entire first night we met and learned we had a lot in common and I thought at the very least we would end up becoming friends."

"And although we lived on opposite sides of the country we kept in touch over the next year through frequent phone calls. It was becoming quite clear that our relationship was becoming serious," especially when Michael decided to pack up and move to Atlanta to be with me," says EJ.

"I guess you could say it was a leap of faith on both our parts but it just felt like the right thing to do, so we purchased a home and began living our lives together. It was also reassuring to know that we had the support of our family and friends", says Michael. "My friends and family were very enthusiastic and EJ's family embraced me as if I were a part of the family."

"We were very lucky but we were also very smart to establish a friendship in the midst of a growing relationship."

"After being together for over a decade we don't always agree with each other on everything but we work to understand each other's feelings which makes it easier to navigate through challenges," says EJ. People often get so serious and caught up in the "relationship" that they forget about being friends. EJ and I genuinely like each other and we laugh and joke with and about each other."

"Our relationship is special and unique and we celebrate our uniqueness and never take each other for granted."

"He must learn to love himself. He must be proud of who he is. He must live an authentic life. And if others cannot accept him then he must accept himself and demand the respect he should have."-Jeffrey Gardere

Doug & Gregory Cooper Spencer

Cooper Spencer Images

"The deeply rooted notion that being a SGL person is antithetical to black progress keeps so many of us at odds with what we can be. It seeps into so many aspects of our lives, quite often in ways that aren't realized. Gay is wrong. Black is right. Black and gay- uh, uh. It's deeply rooted so a lot of black SGL people struggle with the idea. Me? I deconstructed that theory decades ago, so I'm free of all that mess."-Doug

Location: Cincinnati, Ohio

Together twelve years

If there ever was an example of the love which can flourish between two black same gender loving men when societal expectations and toxic theology are deconstructed and exposed as a hindrance towards the pursuit of happiness that we all deserve, then Doug Cooper Spencer 56, and Gregory Cooper Spencer 29, are that very example. With twenty-seven years separating the two in age along with life experiences, the relationship Doug initially envisioned as a mentor was admirable but clearly no match for what the universe had planned or the sight of Greg's legs passing by that caused Doug to stop dead in his tracks.

"We met in downtown Cincinnati on Fountain Square, which is a beautiful plaza in the center of downtown," says Doug. I was amused when I noticed he was interested in me because it was evident he was much younger. I decided to get up and leave so I wouldn't give Greg a chance to come on to me. I'd already been in a relationship that lasted fifteen years and I was eager to live my life alone, so I wasn't really in the mood for another relationship at the time-if at all again."

"At the same moment I made up my mind to leave, he got up the nerve to introduce himself. I immediately told him I knew his intentions and that he was gay and coming on to me. At this point he froze and this look of grave fear came on his face.

That's when my heart sank, because I saw a young man struggling with keeping his sexuality a secret. I immediately wanted to befriend him, like a big brother, to mentor him."

"Our friendship immediately blossomed," says Greg. That night Doug drove me home with the sunroof open. As I got out of the car to walk inside, I leaned over and asked, "Can I see you again?" he mumbled "Yeah". That was the beginning of our six-month courtship that would turn into a serious relationship and eventually marriage. But that was after I came clean about my actual age."

"He was actually seventeen when we met and would be turning eighteen in two months. I told him to come back in two months," laughs Doug.

"I was adamant and called him the entire two months we were apart," says Greg. "On my eighteenth birthday we met up for dinner and the rest is history."

Doug actually gave me the freedom to search around for someone else in order to make sure this is what I wanted. After two years into the relationship and me not having changed my mind we bought a house together and twelve years later our love is still going strong."

"We seriously care about each other's well-being and we work hard to stay together," says Doug. Our relationship is successful because we respect each other and Greg is not only my lover but my best friend."

"I could not imagine walking away from all Doug and I have accomplished together," says Greg. "I love my black husband!"

"If I could take all my parts with me when I go somewhere, and not have to say to one of them, 'No, you stay home tonight, you won't be welcome, because I'm going to an all-white party where I can be gay, but not Black'. Or I'm going to a Black poetry reading and half of the poets are anti-homosexual, or thousands of situations where something of what I am cannot come with me. The day all the different parts of me can come along, we would have what I would call a revolution." – Pat Parker

In Conclusion

As I conclude writing this book, I am overcome by many emotions, such as: gratitude, hope, joy, and many others. I am filled with gratitude and appreciation to the 18 couples who were generous and marvelously unselfish in sharing their stories of love with me. These couples shared the same conviction as I did that it was critically important to show the world and other same-gender loving people of color that there were many other individuals who found loving partners who reciprocated and returned their love and affection. I was also pleased to discover that many of these couples were men of faith who truly loved God and invited God into their relationship. My hope is that their example will disprove the foolish belief that the ideals of loving God and loving the same gender are in opposition to each other.

In my writing this book, which was truly a labor of love, about the joy of same gender love, I became aware of three romantic principles which were recurrent in the stories all of the couples.

The first romantic principle being the strong need for communication between each partner in order to maintain a healthy and vibrant relationship. Some couples even resolved to not go to bed mad until they worked out whatever problem was affecting their relationship.

The second romantic principle was the desire of each partner to put their partner's happiness above their own. This is certainly indicative of lovers raising their ability to compromise to a deeper offering of love. As evidenced by one person's admission, " I would rather be happy then right!"

The third and final romantic principle involves continued investment into the relationship such as the principle of a weekly date night. Many times, relationships wither, atrophy and die because of neglect, whether benign or intentional. Whenever the participants in the relationship stop investing into the relationship, it only a matter of time before, devotion, (which is the glue that holds the relationship together) disintegrates and thus dies the relationship. Date night is a wonderful way to keep your lover close to you emotionally and intimately and keep your relationship strong. In fact, the President Of the United States and the First Lady schedule Date nights on a regular basis.

It is with great hope and eager anticipation that I share this chronicle of love with you, and it is also my profound hope and prayer that you experience the same type of romantic fulfillment when love takes over.

When Love Takes Over

Verse !

when your eyes met mine
for that very first time
I felt the connection
of love's perfection
I tried to resist you
until I kissed you
You sent my senses reeling
Now I can't deny my feelings
when love takes over

Verse 2

after so many heartbreaks
after so many mistakes
I thought love had passed me by
I thought why should I even try
Then God sent you to me
And I took the time to see
how your really do complete me
now I surrender freely
When love takes over

Chorus
when love takes over
your life begins anew
when love takes over
there's nothing you can do
but share your heart and all of your soul
with that one person who makes you whole
life is so sweet because now you're complete
when loves takes over

Bridge
Safe in in your arms I knew I'd be
Wrapped in your love now the world can see
there's nothing wrong with you loving me
where there's true love there's no hypocrisy
When love takes over

love bucket